New England's WITCHES AN

D1048177

This book is dedicated to Mabel Ellis Cahill,
who early in life peaked the author's interest in witches, fortune-tellers,
mystics, and wizards.

Author Bob Cahill at cemetery plot for the Hathorne family, Old
Burying Grounds, Charter Street, Salem, MA - Note, the brass plaque
for the grave of Witch Hanging Judge John Hathorne, is missing. It
was thought to be stolen, but was found in the Salem Police Station
across the street. Photo by Mike Chandler.

Cover Photo: ISBN: 0-916787-00-1

The witch trial of Sarah Good, re-enacted many times each day at
the Witch Dungeon Museum, Salem, Massachusetts. Photo, courtesy
Witch Dungeon.

INTRODUCTION

I don't believe I am any more or less superstitious than anyone else, but I have always been keenly interested in unusual occurrences, unexplained incidents, and unsolved mysteries, in particular those that took place in my native New England.

I was born and brought up in Salem, Massachusetts where, less than 300 years ago, falsely accused and self-proclaimed witches instilled fear and mass hysteria into my hometown and neighboring villages. Today, Salem and her neighboring cities - especially Lynn and Boston - have attracted self-proclaimed witches into our society. On occasion they are all written up in local newspapers and accepted for what they are, or profess to be, but for the most part they are ignored.

Fortune tellers, like witches, are a minority group here in New England, but through attrition have obtained equal rights and are no longer persecuted. Their lot in the days of yore, however, was less brutal than that of the witches. They were merely asked to leave town; whereas, a witch was either hanged or, in the case of Giles Corey, crushed to death.

Ghosts, sea monsters, and visitors from outer space have not yet made it in today's society. A few people may accept their existence, but most scoff at their mere mention. I am not a scoffer, for I have met a ghost - or think I have, about which I will tell you in the Ghostly Haunts book. Also there is concrete evidence mounting to establish the existence of sea monsters. Over 1,000 people saw the sea serpent off the Massachusetts coast back in the 1800's, and that is more than the number who claim to have seen Nessie in Loch Ness.

Many New Englanders have recently reported seeing flying saucers; some say they have had encounters with the so-called little men who pilot these versatile spheres; and two New Hampshire folk insist that they were taken captive by little people from another planet. Few, however, have heard about the visitors who harrassed the villagers of Gloucester in 1692 while the witch trials were going on in Salem. The Gloucester folks of the 17th century called these visitors "the Devil's disciples," and that was their way of explaining away the unknown and the mysterious. Today, there are still many incidents that are not understood, or are so bizarre that they border on incredible; incidents that we usually brush aside as figments on someone's warped imagination, or try to explain as products of mass hysteria. Some, of course, are just that: creations of a fearful society gone mad. One of the stories you will read in this classic series is "The Days the World Ended," about a group of 19th century New Englanders who sold their land holdings and all personal possessions to prepare for Judgment Day, which - unfortunately for them - never came.

New England is also ripe with sea lore, but I have omitted the legend here and collected only unusual, factual stories that are well documented. During my twenty-five years of research, I made some startling discoveries, such as the macabre fate of all ships given the name Atlantic. I have also added a couple of stories about eccentric people whose obssessions, personalities, physical makeup or experiences conflicted with the norm. I do not try to fully explain their madness or idiosyncracies, nor the reasons for any odd occurences. Neither do I attempt to solve the many mysteries presented here -- I leave these puzzling incidents for you to wrestle with in your own mind. I have merely collected stories about local places that I know and love. Some are humorous, others are terrifying, and most boggle the mind. Witches and Wizards is the first in this series.

Bob Cahill

Boston's Irish Witch, Goody Glover.
Sketch by Trish Cahill, courtesy, Witch Dungeon Museum, Salem, MA.

I.
ISSAC CUMMINGS' NIGHTMARE

That a witch or a wizard was entering Issac Cummings' barn each night and stealing off with his horse to a witch meeting in the woods, neither Issac, nor his friends and family had any doubt. The horse was bewitched. "It acted strangely and wouldn't stand up at all during the day," he reported to the magistrates at Salem during the Witch Trials of 1692. It was Issac's brother who decided that Bridget Bishop, who lived nearby, rode it through the sky to the secret demonic meetings, because the horse was faster than a broomstick.

She would return the weary mare to the stable each morning, just before daybreak. It was Issac's brother who also suggested to him that he call in a good animal wizard to break the "wicked witch's curse" on the horse. Of course, this could only be done on a Sunday, the only day that the witches did not ride.

Thomas Andrews of Boxford was not only an animal doctor, but he had been fairly successful, in the past, in breaking demonic curses and witch spells on dogs, cats, and cows. Issac Cummings decided to call him down to Salem to see if he could save his horse. Issac's testimony before the witch court is as follows:

"Andrews decided to try a pipe full of lit tobacco injected into the horse's rump as a cure. I went to the barn, and Andrews did use the pipe as he said he would. The pipe tobacco did blaze and burn blue. Then I said to Andrews, 'You shall try no more, for it is not lawful to do so on the Sabbath.' "

" 'I will try again once more,' said Andrews, which he did. "And then there arose a blaze from the pipe of tobacco," said Issac, "which seemed to me to cover the buttocks of the mare. The blaze went upwards towards the roof of the barn, and in the roof of the barn there was a great crackling, as if the barn would have fallen or been burnt . . . I told Andrews that I would rather lose the mare than the barn, and wanted no more magic done on the Sabbath." The mare, however, stood up immediately and seemingly was cured.

This story was told originally by Robert Calef, who was one of the first to denounce the witchcraft trials. He titled his story, "The Burning Of The Mare's Fart." (Records of Salem Witchcraft Volume II, page 80.)

BOSTON'S IRISH WITCH

Many people have written about the infamous witch trials in Salem and there are varied theories as to how and why this mania began. Usually Tituba, the self-acclaimed witch from the West Indies who lived at Salem Village in 1692, is blamed. Also, the young girls who practiced palmistry at Samuel Parris' parsonage are often accused of starting the hysteria. Actually, the seeds of witchcraft were shown in Massachusetts in 1688, by a powerful Irish witch named Goody Glover.

Mrs. Glover, a hag-like creature, lived in Boston and was emloyed as a laundress. Her husband had died many years before, but before he died, he complained that his wife was a witch. "Wherever my head was laid, she would quickly arrive unto the punishments due to such a one," he said. One blustery winter evening, the four children of Mrs. Glover's neighbor, John Goodwin, accused her of stealing some of their fine linen. Mrs. Glover swore at them and walked away, but the two Goodwin girls and their two brothers "were horribly taken with fits," reported Cotton Mather. Dr. Thomas Oakes of Boston was called in to cure the children and relieve them of their pain, however his medicines had no effect.

"All four children (aged 8 thru 13) were tormented in the same part of their bodies at the same time," reported Cotton Mather in his book MAGNALIA CHRISTI. "Their pain flew like swift lightening from one part to another, and they were kept so far asunder that they neither saw nor heard each other's complaints. When the next day came, they were most miserably handled," said Mather. "Sometimes they were deaf, sometimes dumb, and sometimes blind, and often all this at once. Their tongues would be drawn down their throats and then pulled out upon their chins to a prodigious length. Their mouths were forced open to such a wideness that their jaws were out of joint . . . and the like would happen to their shoulder-blades, their elbows and wrists . . . their necks would be broken, so that their neck-bone would seem dissolved unto them . . . their heads would be twisted almost round . . . and if their friends at any time obstructed a dangerous motion which they seemed upon, they would roar exceedingly . . ."

After two days of such antics by the Goodwin children, the self-esteemed excorcist of the Commonwealth, Cotton Mather, was called in to drive out the evil spirits. He gave them temporary relief and immediately had Mrs. Glover placed in jail.

"It was not long before this woman was brought upon her trial," reported Cotton Mather, "but then the court could have no answers from her but in the Irish, which was her native language, although she understood English very well . . ."

An interpreter was hired by the court and astounded all those present when he revealed that Mrs. Glover did not deny being a witch, rather, she was very proud to be one. Her home was searched, and found under her bed were several puppets made of rags and stuffed with goat's hair. The puppets were presented as evidence at the trial, and Mrs. Glover explained that she would spit on the "images" and stroke them with her hand to send the children into their fits. She demonstrated her ritual before the court and immediately the four Goodwin children who were present "fell into sad fits before the whole assembly."

When the judges asked Goody Glover if she knew of anyone who would defend her, she replied that she had one man who would defend her, "my prince." Then she became angry that her so-called "prince" did not appear, and, as Cotton Mather said, "she was heard expostulating with the devil for his thus deserting her . . . ."

Another neighbor of Mrs. Glover, a Mrs. Hughes, testified against her stating that one woman named Howen was "cruely bewitched to death, about six years before, by Mrs. Glover." Before her death, Mrs. Howen told Mrs. Hughes that Goody Glover "sometimes would come down her chimney." As Mrs. Hughes made her derogatory statements before the Court, her teenaged son was taken ill and began acting much like the Goodwin children had. He cried out at night that a black person in a blue cape danced around his room and tortured him. Mrs. Glover readily admitted that she disguised herself as a black person in a blue cape to frighten the boy, but that she would torture him no more.

Mrs. Glover then told Cotton Mather, "I used to be at meetings where my prince and four others were present." "She entertained me with nothing but Irish," said Reverend Mather, "which language I had not learning enough to understand . . . . When she declined answering some things that I asked her, she told me she could give me full answers, but her spirit would not give her leave . . . . However, against her will I prayed with her, which if it were a fault, it was in my excess of pity. When I had done this," said Mather, "she thanked me with many good words, but I was no sooner out of her sight than she took a stone, a long and slender one, and with her finger and spittle fell to tormenting it."

Goody Glover was hanged a few days later, but before her execution she said that the Goodwin children would not be relieved by her death, and that they would continue to be afflicted by other witches. True to her word, as Cotton Mather put it, "the children continued in their furnace as before, and it grew rather seven times hotter than before the Irish woman's death."

Goody Glover kindled the flame that set Salem ablaze with fear and hatred four years later, and before it was over, hundreds were falsely accused and twenty were executed as witches. One who escaped the hangman's noose was Tituba, who, like Goody Glover, professed to being a witch. Unlike Goody Glover, however, Tituba struck such fear into the hearts of the magistrates that they did not dare take her to Gallows Hill. If poor Mrs. Glover, who was probably demented from old age and an exceedingly hard life, had not been so proud of her witchcraft, there might never have been a Salem Witch.

Sketch, Trish Cahill, courtesy, Witch Dungeon Museum, Salem, Massachusetts.

Sir William Phips, Governor of Massachusetts - The treasure hunting knight who saved the ladies in distress.

III
PHIPS AND THE FORTUNE TELLER

James and Mary Phips of Bristol, Maine had their 21st child on February 2, 1651. They named him William, and proceeded to have five more children after him. When William was in his teens, he decided to run away from home. Unlike his 20 brothers, he did not like farming and sheep herding with his father in Bristol. He wanted to lead an adventurous life, so he took off to Boston. His intention was to go to sea, but instead was persuaded to become an apprentice shipbuilder under John Hull of Boston. When Bill Phips was in his early twenties, he ventured, one evening, to the nearby town of Lynn. Considering a visit to a hag-like fortune teller in Lynn was a lark for Bill and his friends, but her prophecy for Bill haunted him for many years. "Ye will find great riches from the sea", she told him, "and because of it, you will become an influential and successful man. Also, " cackled the old hag, "you will save the likes of me". This prediction convinced Bill Phips to go to sea. At the age of 30, he became skipper of his own ship, trading between Boston and ports in the Caribbean. Tobacco, lumber, molasses, slaves and every other cargo conceivable, Bill and his crew packed aboard, but none of these products gave him the wealth and influence of which the fortune teller had assured him. One get-rich-quick scheme did interest him though. An old native at the port of Haiti had told him about 14 Spanish ships that, in the mid 1600's, had wrecked in a hurricane off Ambrose Bank, Silver Shoals, Bahamas. Some salvagers had found treasure in the shallows there, but it was only a small percentage of the $25,000,000 in gold and silver that was lost in the storm. The ships had been part of the Spanish plate fleet, heading to Spain from Central America.

Bill decided to help fate along. Leaving his new bride behind in Boston, he sailed to London in hopes of convincing King Charles II to back him financially in his quest for treasure. It took Bill a few months to obtain an audience with the King, but Charles II was intrigued by the brash, enthusiastic New Englander, and offered his 22 gun ship ROSE and 100 men for the treasure expedition. The King, of course, would receive the bulk of treasure for providing the transportation, crew, and equipment needed. Phips sailed for the Caribbean in the winter of 1684. He spent months cruising Silver Shoals, dragging a make-shift catch-all behind the ROSE, in hopes of snagging the remains of a shipwreck. The ROSE crew became bored with the routine and began fighting among themselves, to the point of near mutiny. Phips sailed to Port Royal, Jamaica, a noted pirate haven, which four years later sank beneath the sea in an earthquake. There he dumped off his original crew and hired aboard a crew of ex-pirates, offering them a share of whatever treasure was found. His second crew, however, became as restless as the first, and to avoid another mutiny, he sailed the ROSE back to England without a scrap of treasure.

Upon arrival, Phips was plagued with more problems. King Charles II had died in his absence and the new King, James, would have nothing to do with refitting a ship for treasure hunting. In fact, the King, confiscated the ROSE and Bill Phips was thrown into jail as a trouble maker and debtor. Some influential British friends released him. It was these same friends who, after much persuasion by Phips, gave him a new ship, a crew, and provisions to sail back to Silver Shoals. The Duke of Albermearle, Christopher Monck, was the heaviest investor. He provided Phips with two ships, The JAMES AND MARY and the HENRY. Phips decided to use native divers to search the sea bottom this time, instead of his make-shift dragging device, and he sailed to Haiti to obtain them. These men were noted for free diving to 100 foot depths, and for holding their breath underwater for three to four minutes.

Sailing once again around Ambrose Bank, the search was slow and tedious. The native divers splashed in and out of the water for weeks, without finding a trace of sunken Spanish galleons. Phips was 40 years old now, and had never enjoyed the comfort of his home in Boston, where his wife waited patiently for him. "Was the old witch right?" he wondered. "Or am I on a fool's errand?" He questioned himself in his diary.

One warm afternoon as they cruised along the coral bank, Phips spotted a red coral feather in the shallows, and he asked a native diver to retreave it as a present for his wife. The Haitian plunged in and returned to the ship with the feather, shouting excitedly, "big guns down there".

The red coral feather, a form of fan coral, had been growing from the muzzle of a sunken cannon. Cannons were scattered everywhere below, reported the native divers, at depths from 20 to 50 feet. They had found one of the 14 treasure galleons. On the first day of diving, natives returned to the surface with two silver bars, one silver patty the size of a tea cup, and 2,000 silver pieces-of-eight. The JAMES AND MARY and HENRY anchored over the wreck site for some six weeks, during which time, 26 pounds of gold coins and 66,000 pounds of silver bars, patties and coins were salvaged from the decayed Spanish galleon. Although the remains of a second galleon were also found near the first, Phips decided to return to England with the treasure.

The investors and the King's men were there to greet him, and claimed all the treasure, but for one-sixteenth, which went to Phips. The Royal government, however, rewarded Bill with knighthood, and made him first Royal Governor of Massachusetts. Sir William returned to Boston as Governor in 1692 - the fortune teller's prophecy had come true. All, except her added comment that, "you will save the likes of me".

Phips arrived back home just in time to be embroiled in the witch trials and executions of Salem. After his treasure experience, he, of course, believed in witches and soothsayers, but when his own wife was accused of witchcraft, he put an end to the executions at Gallows Hill. It was Governor Phips who liberated 168 people in Salem's Witch Dungeon who were awaiting the hangman's noose. He, as the fortune teller had predicted, "saved the likes of me", and put an end to the witch hysteria. William Phips died at the age of 44, after being Governor for less than three years.

Howard Street Cemetery, behind the Salem Jail, where Giles Corey was crushed to death.

Old Salem Village today, now Danvers, is the site of a recent archaeological dig. Behind the house (below) is where Samuel Parris' and Tituba's house and shanty stood - Items found are on display at the Danvers Historical Society Building on Page Street. This house was the Ingersoll Inn. Across the street from the house is the site of the Puritan Church (above), where another church now stands.

IV
THE CURSE OF GILES COREY

It was a long, bitter cold New England winter in 1691-92. There had not been as much snow in previous winters as far back as anyone at that time could remember. Only four miles from Salem Town was Salem Village (now Danvers), a small community of no more than 100 families; and being so far from the shops and activities of the town, these people had nothing to do but snuggle about the hearth to keep warm for four months. Fireside tales, Biblical readings, and stories of Indian and French massacres helped to pass the time. But for the most part, the people were bored with inactivity, especially the children.

At the parish house of Reverend Samuel Parris, the young girls of the neighborhood enjoyed the palmistry and black magic of a servant woman called Tituba. She and her husband, John Indian, had been slaves who were bought by Mr. Parris, while he was a merchant in the West Indies. Reverend Parris was a strict Biblical scholar, and strict as well with his nine-year old daughter, Elizabeth, and her eleven year old cousin, Abigail Williams, who lived in the parish house. Tituba, on the other hand, was not interested in the Bible, for she practiced and professed voodooism.

As a desired diversion, Elizabeth, Abigail and their friends: Ann Putnam, aged 12; Elizabeth Hubbard; Mary Warren; Mercy Lewis; Mary Walcott; Elizabeth Booth and Susan Sheldon, all in their late teens, sat around the kitchen fire listening to Tituba and John Indian talk of the Devil and his powers.

During the first sessions, the girls giggled a lot and thoroughly enjoyed themselves, all the time realizing that Tituba took the Black Arts seriously. Before long, the impressionable girls were believing what the slave woman told them, and they began participating in her ceremonies, which included deep trances and sinister spells. It is even possible that Tituba had the girls drinking hard cider and taking hallucinogenic drugs that she had brought with her to Salem from the West Indies.

At home, in sight of their parents and other elders of Salem, the girls began performing nightmarish fits; nobody knew how to cope with them, or what caused them. Abigail Williams, for example, "ran to the fire and began to throw fire brands about the house and run against the back as if she would run up the chimney." Elizabeth Parris threw her father's Bible across the living room, an act that, under any other circumstance, would have resulted in a severe beating from the Salem minister.

He was frightened and confused. Each day, Elizabeth and Abigail would double up in convulsions, scream and sob, shout blasphemies and throw things about the house. Abigail usually waited for prayer time in the Parris home to have her fits. Reverend Parris sent Abigail to live with Stephen Sewall, brother of Judge Sewall, who was soon to become deeply involved in the witch trials. This change of atmosphere, however, did not affect Abigail's behavior.

The antics of little Ann Putman, who had a wild imagination, and was probably more taken in with Tituba's tales and teachings than any of the others, immediately convinced her high strung mother that she was the victim of the devil.

Mary Walcott's aunt, Mary Sibley, seemed to take her niece's wild behavior lightly, for she asked young Mary to have John Indian make her a "witch cake." An edible witch cake was made of barley, rye, water and herbs. A witch cake to supposedly cure smallpox, which was raging in 1692, included the above with an added cup of baby's urine. After the cake was baked, it was to fed to the dog. If the dog shuddered when he ate it, the diseased person would supposedly be cured.

Reverend Parris called in the local doctor, Griggs, to examine his daughter and the other girls. The doctor, as Parris himself had already concluded, diagnosed their sickness as "bewitchment," but the doctor had no cure. In order to avoid punishment for their tantrums, the girls were already blaming others in the community for their afflictions. Tituba, of course, became a guilty party, but she readily admitted to being a witch. Others, such as the pipe-smoking beggar, Sarah Good, and the aged cripple Sarah Osborn, were shocked at the accusations. On February 19, 1692, all three were officially charged with witchcraft. They went for examination before the magistrates on March 1, where they first heard the specifics of having "tortured, afflicted, pinned, consumed, wasted, and tormented the young ladies of Salem Village."

If only there was someone in Salem who remembered the case of William Perry, the witch hysteria might have ended then and there. William Perry was a boy from Leicester, England, who, in 1620, had accused an old woman named Jane Clark of being a witch. As in the case of the Salem girls, young William claimed Mrs. Clark provoked him into convulsions. After long hours of questioning by the judges, William Perry admitted that he had contrived the fits and convulsions and had falsely accused the old woman, because he enjoyed all the attention he was getting. The English, however, did not learn from the boy's confession either, for the last English witch to be executed was but seven years before the Salem reign of terror.

At the examination in March, Tituba admitted to teaching the girls the Black Arts and to bewitching them. Then she began accusing other ladies of Salem of being witches. The girls blamed Sarah Good for not only tormenting them, but also for speaking angrily to people, which caused their cows to die. Ann Putnam, now being coaxed by her mother, who was also called Ann, said that Sarah Good had tried to make her sign the Devil's book. This was tantamount to selling one's soul. The girls were present at these so-called examinations, and during the ordeal they continued to screech and roll around on the floor, swooning and sputtering incoherent phrases.

Before sending the women off to jail to await trial, the magistrates had all the girls look each accused witch in the eyes to see if these were definitely the women who bewitched them. They all stared unblinkingly at the old women and said, "these were the ones who did torment us."

The girls were now feeling the power of their play acting and they began accusing others. Two avid churchgoers were next: Rebecca Nurse and Martha Corey, ages 70 and 60. Both were well-respected in the community, although Martha Corey had given birth to an illegitimate son. Mrs. Corey had said, when Tituba and Sarah Good were accused, "I cannot blame the devil for making witches of them, for they are idle, slothful persons and mind nothing that is good." Little did she know that she would be next!

The examinations of Rebecca and Martha were much like those of the three women preceding them, although Rebecca almost convinced the judges that she was not a witch. Ann Putnam's mother, who disliked Rebecca Nurse because of her straight-forwardness, cried out, "Did you not bring the black man with you? Did you not bid me tempt God and die? How often have you eaten and drunk your own damnation?"

"Oh Lord, help me, " cried Rebecca, and at this plea, young Ann screamed that Goody Nurse was biting her. She then showed her bite marks on the wrist to the magistrate. Rebecca, along with Martha Corey, was immediately taken to Salem Jail to await trial.

The trials began when Sir William Phips, the Royal Governor, appointed a special court to try the cases. Presiding justice was William Stoughton, assisted by Samuel Sewall, John Hathorne and Jonathan Corwin. Judge Corwin's nephew, George Corwin who was only 26 years old, was appointed Sheriff of Essex County.

As the trials got under way, a group of Boston ministers, with prominent Cotton Mather as their leader, provided written advice for the judges. "We deplore witchcraft, and all means must be taken to combat the devil and his works," said Mather. He added, "spectral evidence should not be admitted as proof," but spectral evidence was not discredited during the trials. In fact, the judges thrived on it.

It was Ann Putnam again who testified that Reverend George Burroughs had come to her one night as an apparition and wanted her to sign the Devil's books. Two women also appeared to her wearing winding sheets and they scolded the spectre of Burroughs. The ghosts, Ann said, were the minister's first and second wives. They told Ann that George Burroughs had murdered them, and one of them showed her where she was stabbed. On this spectral evidence, Reverend George Burroughs was condemned to the gallows. Burroughs had been a pastor at Salem Village church before Samuel Parris. It had been because of arguments with Ann Putnam's mother that he had left Salem for a parish in Wells, Maine. He was a little man who was very strong; he often displayed his strength by lifting barrels filled with food and liquids, and by holding a heavy musket straight out with one hand. Because of this phenomenal strength, young Ann persuaded the judges to have the Sheriff ride to Maine and carry Reverend Burroughs back to Salem Dungeon in a cart. He was hanged at Gallows Hill in Salem Town on August 19, 1692.

The hysteria increased and spread to other towns and villages. Grudges against neighbors became reason for accusations of witchcraft. Other children, to share in the attention, and revengeful or frightened adults, joined the nine original girls in condemning others. It seemed that almost everyone in Salem suspected someone else of being a witch. Sarah Martin was taken to trial because she managed to step in a mud puddle without getting her shoes and stockings muddied. Two dogs were strung up at Gallows Hill because one of the girls said they had appeared to her as the Devil's disciples, and gave her the evil eye.

John Proctor and his wife, from Salem village, were accused by teenager Mary Warren, their servant girl, who admittedly did not like John. "When Mary was first taken with fits," John said, "I kept her close to the spinning wheel and then she had no more fits." Mary apparently did not like working the spinning wheel. "Using a cudgel on the girls' bottoms," said John Proctor, "would be an effective way of dealing with them." Proctor also commented that if he had Tituba or John Indian in his custody, he'd beat the Devil out of them.

Actually, Mary Warren caused more problems for herself by accusing the Proctors. The five Proctor children were placed under her custody and the over-zealous Sheriff had confiscated all of the Proctors' goods and cattle, leaving no furniture or food in the house for Mary to use in caring for the children. She was the first of the original "afflicted children," as they were called, to weaken, and she told the other girls that she wanted to confess her sins and false accusations to the judges. Immediately, Ann Putnam and Abigail Williams called Mary "a witch." For five weeks the girls threatened her and said they would see to it that she was tortured and placed in the dungeon at Salem Jail. She finally reneged and told the judges that John Proctor had afflicted her, and that his apparition had made her sign the Devil's book.

Sarah Churchill, George Jacobs' 20 year old servant girl, after accusing her master, also tried to defect. She, with Sarah Trask, 19; Martha Sprague, 16; Phoebe Chandler, 12; and Margaret Reddington, 20, sent five members of the Jacobs household to jail. George called them all "witch bitches." When Sarah realized that George Jacobs would hang because of her lies, she decided to confess her ill-doings, but the girls threatened her, as they had Mary Warren, and Sarah changed her mind.

John Proctor and George Jacobs were hanged from the trees at Gallows Hill, along with Reverend Burroughs, on August 19. With them on the gallows that day were John Willard of Salem Village, who had accused the young girls of being witches, and Martha Carrier of Andover, sister of Rebecca Nurse. Mary Lacy of Andover, who admitted to witchcraft, confessed that "me and Martha Carrier did both ride on a stick or pole when we went to witch meetings at Salem Village." Thus, Martha Carrier was condemned to hang and Mary Lacy was saved from the hangman's noose. Ironically, those who confessed to being witches were not executed, but many who denied the girls' stories, or criticized them in court, were hanged. Mary Lacy realized this and, after a few weeks in jail, she confessed to "squeezing and choking dolls" made in the images of a hated neighbor. Her mother, Ann Foster, died in the Dungeon due to ill treatment from Sheriff George Corwin.

William Barker, also from the town of Andover, told the judges that he was a witch and that "the Devil's design was to destroy Salem Village .... to begin at the minister's house .... and to destroy the Church of God to set up Satan's Kingdom." This statement alone was enough to frighten every person in Essex County, especially the judges. Of the 168 people accused of being witches, 55 of them admitted to having made a pact with the Devil, or stated that they were possessed by an evil spirit who forced them into witchcraft.

The girls continued their uncontrollable fits during the trials, pretending trances, swooning, and feigning that certain Devil's disciples were pinching and strangling them. Their tales became even more extraordinary as they quickly became the center of attention and fear in New England. One eyewitness to the trials, Robert Calef, saw through their charade. He later wrote, "The oldest girls assumed sundry odd postures and made antic gestures, uttering foolish ridiculous speeches, which neither they themselves nor any others could make sense of." The disbelievers, however, were in the minority. Spokesmen from almost every town and village for 20 miles around Salem asked that the girls visit their communities, to point out the witches in their midst. The girls gleefully complied with these invitations until the jails could hold no more.

The Salem girls even went so far as to accuse the famous John Alden - son of the Pilgrim - whom Longfellow made famous in his poem. Alden was brought to Salem from Boston to face the girls. "There stands Alden," said one of his accusers, "a bold fellow who sells powder and shot to the Indians and French, and lies with Indian squaws and has Indian papooses." When Alden approached them, they all fainted face down on the courtroom floor. Alden then turned to Judge Hathorne and said, "What's the reason you don't fall when I look at you?" Hathorne had no answer. Alden was imprisoned, but he managed to escape from jail three months later.

Another prominent man of the time, merchant Philip English of Salem, had an "afflicted child's" finger pointed at him, but he did not wait around to face the judges. He skipped town with his wife, who was also accused, and did not return until the hysteria had tempered. He later became a wealthy and prominent leader in Salem.

Of the 31 condemned to death by the judges, 14 women and five men rode in the cart before the public from Prison Lane (now St. Peter Street) in Salem, down Essex and Boston Streets and over the town bridge which led up to Gallows Hill. Many followed them through the streets, shouting and throwing stones at them. Besides Mrs. Foster, Sarah Osborne, one of the first three to be accused, died in the Witch Dungeon from exposure, ill treatment, and lack of adequate food. Abigail Faulkner and Elizabeth Proctor, John's wife, avoided execution because they were pregnant. Five others who were condemned to death, confessed to being witches and were therefore reprieved.

One Sarah Dustin of Reading, who was reprieved, had no close relatives to pay the jail fees she owed for her keep, so she too died of poor health in the Salem Dungeon. Accused witch Mary Bradbury of Salisbury, when condemned to the gallows, managed to escape jail with the help of outsiders. Many relatives, friends and neighbors, at the risk of being accused themselves, came to the aid of the condemned. Over 50 Salem families signed a petition to help the Proctors, but the judges paid no attention. These same people were forced to pay the hangman's fee when John Proctor was executed.

The most tragic and brutal murder in the name of justice was that of Giles Corey. When his wife Martha was accused and imprisoned in the winter of '92, he pleaded with the judges, to no avail, that he be allowed to stay in jail with her. It wasn't long, however, before the girls named him as a witch as well. He was 80 years old when he was called to stand before the court. The courageous old man would not answer any questions, nor would he comment when the girls faced him and made accusations. When asked how he pleaded, "guilty or not guilty," he remained mute. By not pleading one way or the other, English law dictated that a person could not be tried, but the penalty for standing mute was "slow crushing under weights" until a plea was forthcoming or the person died. Although the laws of the Colony read that "for bodily punishment we allow amongst us none that are inhumane, barbarous or cruel," the judges decided to follow English law.

Many of Corey's friends believed he remained silent in court because, by so doing under English law, he could leave his property to whomever he pleased. Otherwise, the Sheriff would confiscate it as he had done with John Proctor's goods and property. Giles was a stubborn, fiery man, who realized he would not get a fair trial. His silence was his way of showing contempt for the "witch bitches" and the judges.

On Monday, September 19, 1692, Giles Corey was led naked to a pit in the open field beside the Salem Jail. He was made to lie down in the pit, then six men lifted heavy stones, placing them one by one, on his stomach and chest. Giles Corey did not cry out, which perplexed Sheriff Corwin, whose duty it was to squeeze a confession from the old man.

"Do you confess?" the Sheriff cried over and over again. More and more rocks were piled onto him, and the Sheriff, from time to time, would stand on the boulders staring down at Corey's bulging eyes. Robert Calef, who was witnessing this torture with many other townfolk, said, "In the pressing, Giles Corey's tongue was pressed out of his mouth; the Sheriff, with his cane, forced it in again."

Only three mouthfuls of bread and three draughts of water were fed to the old man during his many hours of pain. Finally, before he expired, he cried out at the sheriff, "Damn you. I curse you and Salem!" Three days after his death by crushing, his wife Martha was hanged at Gallows Hill.

Giles Corey's cruel death seemed to bring about a change in the feelings of Salemites. The hysteria began to subside somewhat and people sickened of seeing their relatives, friends, and neighbors executed on hearsay.

Young Ann Putnam and her mother, who were truly the ringleaders of this hideous sport, seemed to sense the change in people's attitudes. After Giles Corey's death, they persuaded Tom Putnam, young Ann's father, who was an influential constable, to write a report to the judges.

"Last night, my daughter Ann," he wrote, "was greviously tormented by witches, threatening that she should be pressed to death before Giles Corey; but through the goodness of a gracious God, she had, at last, a little respite. Whereupon there appeared unto her a man in a winding sheet who told her that Giles Corey had murdered him by pressing him to death with his feet; but that the Devil then appeared unto Giles Corey and convenanted with him and promised him that he should not be hanged--It must be done to him as he had done to me . . . ." Tom Putnam's wife also spread the rumor that Giles Corey had beaten a man to death some 16 years earlier and that God had seen to it that he got his deserved punishment.

As hard as Ann and others tried to keep the witch hysteria going, fear of witches was waning. Among other things, the judges were telling the girls to hold their tongues during the trials, and even some of the girls were tiring of the game they were playing.

At Salem's Ingersoll Inn, one girl announced that she saw Mrs. Proctor afflicting guests at the Inn. The owner of the Inn, Mrs. Ingersoll, called the young girl a liar. "But I only said it for sport," admitted the girl. "We must have some sport."

By May of 1693, the girls had reached too high in their pursuit of witches. They accused Lady Phips, wife of the Governor. In that month and year, Governor Phips had all those accused of witchcraft and those who were awaiting execution released from Salem's Witch Dungeon. The hideous prank had cost 23 people their lives.

Some 14 years later, at age 26, Ann Putnam confessed her fraud and had the minister read her confession at Sunday service. "It was a great delusion of Satan that deceived me in that sad time," she said, "whereby I justly fear I have been instrumental to bring upon myself and this land the guilt of innocent blood." Ann, it seems, still blamed the Devil for her actions.

Tituba, the real instigator of the witch dilemna in Salem, spent 14 months in jail and was then sold into slavery to pay her jail expenses. She was the only one of the 168 accused who believed she was a witch, and maybe she was. The only one who profited by the witch trials was Sheriff George Corwin, who confiscated property and pocketed fees collected from the accused and their relatives.

As the writer of this story, I have but one knawing fear concerning George Corwin, the cruel Sheriff of Essex County, and Giles Corey's curse upon him. I was recently elected the Sheriff of Essex County, and Master & Keeper of the Salem Jail. All the High Sheriffs of this county before me, including Corwin, either died in office from heart problems, or retired with an ailment of the blood. Of course, if there are no such things as witch spells and curses, I shouldn't have to worry about Giles Corey's Curse, should I?

> (Robert E. Cahill, the author of this story, suffered a rare blood disease, heart attack, and stroke, in 1978, after writing this piece, and was forced to retire as Sheriff of the County, and as Master and Keeper of the Salem Jail.)

Hanged At Gallows Hill, Salem — 1692

Name	Village Or Town	Date Of Hanging
1. Bridget Bishop	Salem	June 10
2. Sarah Good	Salem Village (Danvers)	July 19
3. Susanna Martin	Amesbury	July 19
4. Elizabeth Howe	Ipswich	July 19
5. Rebecca Nurse	Salem Village (Danvers)	July 19
6. Sarah Wildes	Topsfield	July 19
7. George Jacobs	Salem Village (Danvers)	August 19
8. Martha Carrier	Andover	August 19
9. George Burroughs	Wells, Maine	August 19
10. John Proctor	Salem Village (Peabody)	August 19
11. John Willard	Salem Village (Danvers)	August 19
12. Martha Corey	Salem Village (Peabody)	Sept. 22
13. Mary Easty	Topsfield	Sept. 22
14. Alice Parker	Salem	Sept. 22
15. Mary Parker	Andover	Sept. 22
16. Ann Pudeater	Salem	Sept. 22
17. Wilmot Reed	Marblehead	Sept. 22
18. Margaret Scott	Rowley	Sept. 22
19. Samuel Wardwell	Andover	Sept. 22

Most Of The Salem Witches Were Not From Salem

Most of the accused in 1692, came from Andover and Salem Village, which is now Danvers and Peabody, Massachusetts. Only ten people were accused of witchcraft in Salem Towne. The following is a list by village and town of the number of men and women accused of witchcraft in 1692-93, who went before the magistrates for examination and or trial:

Andover	38	Marblehead	2
Boxford	2	Lynn	7
Boston ·	1	Malden	1
Amesbury	1	Reading	4
Billerica	6	Rowley	1
Beverly	6	Romney Marsh (Revere)	1
Charlestown	3	Salisbury	1
Chelmsford	1	Salem	10
Gloucester	3	Salem Village (Danvers & Peabody)	30
Haverhill	3	Topsfield & Ipswich	7
Great Island	1	Wells, Maine	1
		Woburn	3

In addition to the 134 listed above, another 34 were accused and in various jails, notably Salem's Witch Dungeon, awaiting examination and or trial, when the General Court released them.

V
THE POWER OF WITCHCRAFT

"God will give you blood to drink," was the curse of Matthew Maule, a Salem Puritan, who was about to hang at Gallows Hill. The curse was directed to Gilbert Pyncheon, a wealthy merchant, who accused Maule of witchcraft because he owned a fresh water spring, which he had refused to sell to Pyncheon. After Maule was executed, Pyncheon bought the land on which the spring was located and built a gabled mansion beside it. A few years later, Gilbert Pyncheon was found dead in one of the upstairs rooms of the mansion. He died of hemorrhage - "drowned in his own blood," as one writer put it. The old mansion is still standing on Turner Street in Salem and is visited by over 100,000 people every year - tourists, anxious to see the upstairs room where Gilbert Pyncheon fell victim to Maule's curse. The mansion is the House of Seven Gables, made famous by Nathaniel Hawthorne's novel of the same name. Most people read Hawthorne's book as fiction, however the curse itself was not made up by Hawthorne. When writing about it, he knew it was very real. In fact, the curse had been directed at his own family.

Judge John Hathorne, Nathaniel's great-great grandfather was Salem's "witch hanging judge," who was often cursed by accused witches as they were about to face the gallows. When Rebecca Nurse, a religious, God-fearing woman, was condemned as a witch by the Court in Salem, the jury, in a surprise move, repreaved her; nonetheless Hathorne insisted that she be hanged. As members of the jury changed their minds for the second time, Rebecca gave Judge Hathorne "the evil eye," and shouted, "I curse you and your blood forever." When Bridget Bishop was condemned, she bestowed a similar curse on Judge Hathorne, adding, "If I am a witch, you'll soon know it." Sarah Good, a pipe smoking begger woman who shared the hanging tree with Rebecca Nurse, cursed Reverend Noyes as the rope was about to be tightened around her neck - "I'll give you blood to drink," she shouted at him; Noyes died years later of blood hemorrhage - thus Nat Hawthorne had enough factual material to write his masterpiece of fiction. While attending Bowdoin college, Nat changed his name officially from Hathorne to Hawthorne, but he never gave reason why. Some of his friends said it was because he was ashamed of what Judge Hathorne did; but others insisted it was because of the curse on the family Hathorne.

There is dispute to this day about whether or not Bridget Bishop was a witch, or merely another innocent victim hanged at Gallows Hill in 1692. At her trial she insisted, "I am innocent. I know nothing about witchcraft, and I don't even know what a witch is?" This, however, wasn't Bridget's first time in Salem Court for the crime of witchcraft. In 1679, John Ingerson's black slave testified that he had seen "the shape of her upon a beam in the barn, holding an egg," presumably to put a hex on Ingerson and his farm animals. She was also accused of bewitching her first husband, a Mr. Wasslebee, to death; and her second husband, Thomas Oliver, considered her a witch. She was then acquitted, only to be tried and found guilty of witchcraft 13 years later. Bridget Bishop was the first to be hanged at Gallows Hilll in 1692. At this trial, her third husband, Edward Bishop, testified that, "she sat up all night long with the Devil."

Bridget was a tavern owner. Her "ordinary" was on the road between Salem and Beverly, now Bridge Street; there she served "a new vile liquid called rum", which Salem sailors drank in vast quantities. The sailors also played an evil game called "shuffleboard" at her tavern, often until very late at night. Bridget was not pretty and she had a sharp tongue, but, for some reason, men were attracted to her. The church fathers, however, only came to see her to reprimand her for her activities and the women of the Puritan church, of course, despised her. She also wore bright and colorful clothes - a practice shunned by the Puritans who then ruled Massachusetts Bay with an iron hand. When the young girls accused her of being a witch, few people of Salem were surprised. Most, in fact, had long ago concluded that she was a witch.

One to speak out against Bridget was Samuel Gray, who said that she killed his new born child. "I saw her spectre come into my room and visit the baby's crib," he told the court. "I looked up and saw the woman with something between both hands, holding it before my mouth . . . Something cold came to my lips . . . The child in the cradle gave a great screech, as if it were greatly hurt, and she disappeared . . . . from which time, the child did pine away. . . . It lived some months after, and so died. Yet both her garb and countenance doth testify that it was the same woman that they now call Bridget Bishop, alias Oliver, of Salem."

A neighbor, Samuel Shattuck, testified that Bridget turned his son into a vegetable. His wife had had an argument with Bridget over medicine Bridget had recommended for the sickly seven year old child; the wife had also accused Bridget of stealing money from the Shattuck house. "The child then," said Sam Shattuck, "suffered an unknown disease". Samuel was convinced that the child was bewitched. The only cure for the sickness was to "draw blood from the witch's face," which would break the curse. He sent the child with an older friend to Bridget's house, where, understanding their mission, Bridget chased them off -

threatening to hit them over the head with a shovel. In the brief skirmish, as the child attempted to scratch Bridget's face, she, instead, scratched his. "And ever since, " said the father, "this child hath been followed with grievous fits . . . head and eyes drawn aside so as if they would never come to rights again"; within a few months time, the child became an idiot.

Two other neighbors, the Coman brothers, Richard and William, said that Bridget's spectre visited Richard for two nights in a row, and tried to "lay atop of me while my wife slept." On the third night, with William in the bedroom carrying a sword for protection, Bridget appeared again, "and took hold of me by the throat and almost hauled me out of bed" . . . . William was immediately struck speechless and could not move hand or foot, and she tried to take William's sword from him . . . . "Also my wife and Sarah Phillips, that lay with my wife, who told me afterwards they had heard me but had not power to speak or stir . . . and the witch vanished."

John Louder, a boarder at John Gedney's house, next door to Bridget's home, added a few verbal nails to help close the lid on the accused witch's coffin. He had argued with Bridget about her chickens coming into Gedney's garden, "and some little time after which, about the dead of night, I felt a great weight upon my breast. I awakened and did clearly see said Bridget Bishop, or her likeness, sitting upon my stomach. She presently laid hold of my throat and almost choked me, and I had not strength or power in my hands to resist to help myself. In this condition she held me to almost day." Louder went on to testify during the April, 1692 court session, that, "some time after that I, not being well, stayed at home on the Lord's Day; the door being shut, I did see a black pig in the room coming towards me. So I went towards it to kick it and it vanished away. Immediately after, I did see a black thing jump into the window, and it came and stood before my face. The body of it looked like a monkey, only the feet were like a cock's feet with claws, and the face somewhat more like a man's than a monkey's . . . . Upon which I cried out, 'The whole armour of God be between me and you!' So it sprung back and flew out over the appletrees, flinging the dust with its feet. It also shook many apple off from the tree."

Bridget Bishop said at her trial that she didn't know John Louder, but she could not deny knowing John and Willie Bly, for she had earlier called on them to repair a crumbling wall in the cellar of her home. What they said they found hidden behind the cellar wall, was literally the final straw that broke dear Bridget's neck. "Several puppets," the Bly brothers testified under oath, "made up of rages, straw, and hog's bristles, with headless pins in them."

When Bridget Bishop was "dragged up Prison Lane under guard," wrote Cotton Mather, on her way to the court house to hear the verdict of death by hanging, "a strange thing happened." She gave an evil look toward the Puritan Meeting House, America's first Protestant Church, which stood at, what is now, Town House Square. "Immediately," said Mather, "a demon, invisible, entering the meeting house, tore down part of it. . . . The people, at the noise, running in, found a board which was strongly fastened with several nails, transported into another quarter of the house."

Was Bridget Bishop an evil person, possibly a prostitute, or even a murderess? or was she just an outspoken, rebellious innocent, under the watchful eye of a Puritanical society? Or, was she really a practicing witch? We'll never really know the answer, but she had power in the community, a power that her neighbors feared. During the 17th century, just about everyone believed in witches and their evil powers. To them, there was no doubt that Bridget Bishop was a witch. Even today, witchcraft can be very powerful stuff - for those who believe in it.

Finding the puppets in Bridget's cellar made her guilt undeniable, as it had Boston's Irish Witch, Goody Glover, some four years before. As Cotton Mather wrote, "orders were given to search the old woman's house, whence there were brought into the court, several small images, or puppets, or babies, made of rags and stuffed with goat's hair and other such ingredients. When these were produced, the vile woman acknowledged that her way to torment the objects of her malice was by wetting of her fingers with the spittle and stroking of those little images."

It is obvious that Judge Hathorne believed in the power of puppets in witchcraft. He actually demonstrated that power in the courtroom during the examination of an accused witch, a black slave named Candy, who, like Tituba, came from Barbados. "Yes, I am a witch," Candy told Hathorne, adding, "my mistress Mrs. Hawkes made me a witch." Candy asked permission to leave the court for a few minutes so she could run home and bring her puppets back to the courtroom. Hathorne agreed, and she returned with "a handkerchief, wherein several knots were tied; rags of cloth; a piece of cheese and a piece of grass." The Judge made Candy eat the grass and cheese. He then ordered her to burn the handkerchief and rags, which she did, "burning herself in the flesh." Candy screamed and dropped the flaming cloth to the courtroom floor; Hathorne quickly picked it up to dunk it into a jug of water to extinquish the flames. Then, one of the accusing girls who was present in the court "tried to rush to the nearby river, as if she would drown herself." One wonders why, after producing such dramatic results with the burning handkerchief, Judge Hathorne himself wasn't accused of witchcraft.

Another witch tool, or charm, which is today synonymous with fortune telling, was the round bottle or crystal ball. Reverend John Hale of Beverly, during the Salem witch trials, was a zealous witch hunter until his wife was accused. He wrote a "Modest Enquiry", in which he states, "I knew of one of the afflicted persons who did try with an egg and a glass to find her future husband's calling, till there came up a coffin (in the glass). She was afterwards followed with diabolical molestations to her death, and so died a single person. . . . Another I was called to pray with, being under sore fits and vexations of Satan, upon examination I found that she had tried the same charm." Hale also writes about his neighbor, Dorcas Hoar, who found guilty at the Salem trials as "a known worshiper of the occult . . . . borrowed a book on palmistry and told people's fortunes and read their palms. She foretold a poor woman's husband's death," wrote Hale.

Samuel Wardwell, at his examination for suspected witchcraft in Salem, admitted that, "I tell fortunes, which sometimes come to pass." He was hanged. His wife, however, claimed to practice witchcraft for many years after 1692, but the authorities did not molest her.

Collecting other people's urine, as nurses do today when one goes for a physical checkup, was used by witches to put curses on specific persons or, if collected by a victim, as a counter--charm against a witch. As mentioned earlier in this book, Mary Sibley, aunt of one of the afflicted girls, had John Indian, Tituba's husband, make a "witch cake" in which the basic ingredient was baby urine. Reverend Samuel Parris said that, "until the making of the witch cake, there was no suspicion of witchcraft." Thomas Maule, possibly the man who provided Nat Hawthorne with the name for "Maule's Curse" in his novel, believed that boiling urine was a countercharm to witchcraft. In the Winter of 1682, he was bothered by rocks constantly hitting his house, thrown by unseen hands, and obviously the work of witches or wizards. He, "set on the fire a pot with urine and crooked pins in it, with designs to have it boil and, by that means, to give punishment to the wizard." He revealed this during an earlier Salem trial, accusing a neighbor of witchcraft. "As the liquor began to grow hot," he said, "a stone came and broke the top of the pot, and threw it down and spilt what was in it; which being made good again, another stone, as the pot grew hot again, broke the handle off; and being recruited and filled the third time, was then, with a third stone, quite broke to pieces and spilt. So," Maule concluded, "the operation became frustrate and fruitless."

At about the same time Thomas Maule was trying to boil his "charming" urine soup, a local doctor named Roger Toothaker told his neighbor Thomas Gage that his daughter had actually killed a witch, using the witch's own urine as a counter charm. Miss Toothaker waited, hidden in the bushes, until the witch visited her outhouse, then, when the witch left, she collected samples of her urine. She brought it back to her home and boiled it in an earthen pot in the fireplace. Although, as Doctor Toothaker revealed to Gage, the thick smelly smoke blocked up the fireplace flu, next morning, the witch was dead. Wilmot "Mammy" Reed, witch of Marblehead, cursed her neighbor, a Mrs. Simms, with the words, "may you never urinate or carcare again," and, at the Salem witch trials, Mrs. Simms confessed that after receiving the curse, she couldn't pee for weeks. She did not mention carcare. John Willard's own grandfather testified at Salem that, "when Willard came into my house, I could not dine or eat anything. I cannot express the misery I was in, for my water suddenly stopped, and I had no benefit of nature but was like a man in a rock. I told my wife immediately," said the old man, "that Willard had done me wrong . . . . then I was taken with the sorest distress and misery, my water being turned into real blood." Mammy Reed and John Willard swung from the tree at Salem's Gallows Hill.

To work their magic or bestow a curse, witches used a variety of herbs and plants, most of them growing in their own gardens. Even before a witch could ride through the air on a broomstick, she would have to anoint herself and the stick with magical ointments. The beautiful flowering plant called "monkshood", rubbed over the witch's body, allowed her to fly, thought some Colonials, or "belladonna", which, if ingested, certainly would give her the sensation of flying, for it is a narcotic which causes delirium. Eating the brain of a cat, so some of our ancestors thought, would produce the same results. The "smallage plant" was used to prevent a flying witch from getting cramps; to get the broom off the ground, the witch had to rub it with a mixture of parsnip juice, aconite, nightshad, baby fat (animal fat would do, but the witch couldn't fly as high and would have to maneuver around tall tress) and soot from the fireplace.

As silly as all this may sound, many suspected witches of early New England aquired a profound knowledge of the affects of herbs and plants, as handed down from mother to daughter, through many generations. Great Stambridge, Essex, England, is still called "The Witch Country;" where there were and still are, many marvelous remedies for various sicknesses, as well as old legends of female witchdoctors who transformed themselves into animals and flew on sticks around the Essex Marsh. These legends and wonder drugs crossed the Atlantic in the early 1600s, to be retold and replanted in America, especially in Essex County, Massachusetts, and its shire town of Salem.

Alse Young of Connecticut was convicted of witchcraft, after she had given a prescription to help a sick child which resulted in harmful side effects. She was hanged as America's first condemned witch in 1647. A year later, Margaret Jones of Charlestown, Massachusetts, for giving neighbors various remedies for sickness, was hanged at Boston Common. Caribbean slaves, such as, Tituba, Candy, and John Indian, brought witch legends and their own kind of magical cures and curses to New England. Also, the Indians who were living here when the Puritans came had their embellished tales and works of wonder, that influenced Colonial America. Cotton Mather in his "Memorable Providences," states that, "the Indians here worship the Devil," and that, "in their powaws, often raise their masters in the shapes of bears and snakes and fires." The plant "wolfbane" is a poison used by witches, but was also smeared on the tips of arrows by American Indians to numb the senses of their victims.

The common wild rye grasses of New England often caused cows to get sick, but a witch could cure any animal sickness with "marshwort". If she wanted to make a human feel sick, however, she'd mix the rye grass with the victim's food in some clever undetected manner. Too much of the rye grass, or an intended overdose, would cause fits and possibly blindness to the witch's prey. There is even a popular theory today that mouldy rye was the real cause of the Salem witch hysteria. An article in "Science-Magazine," of April 2, 1976, by Linda Caporael, a University of California graduate student, reveals that the physical afflictions of the accusing girls, might have been caused by "Convulsive Ergotism", a disorder resulting from the ingestion of contaminated rye grain. "Rye, which grows in low, wet ground, yields ergot," wrote Miss Caporael. Judge Sewall's diary states that before the rye was harvested for the 1692 season, to be eaten in Salem in bread and cereals, "it was rainy and warm, hot and stormy." Ergot (claviceps purpura), according to Doctor John Stearns, the man who discovered the fungus in 1807, "causes symptoms of hallucination, violent fits, choking, pinching, itching, a crawling sensation in the skin, and muscular contractions." Linda Caporael adds that "females and children are more likely to get ergot poisoning than males." It is interesting to note that John Indian's "witch cake" not only had baby urine as an ingredient, but rye grains as well. If ergot was the cause of the Salem witch hysteria, and even if the people of Salem had discovered that their rye was possibly poisoned, witches would still have been deemed responsible, and it probably would not have changed the gruesome outcome in 1692 Salem.

The witch's poison and the witch's touch were her most powerful weapons. The poisonous "H" group, "hemlock, henbane and hemp," were what Colonials feared most. A small dose of hemlock causes excitement, but a larger dose can paralyze a person; henbane can kill; and hemp is one of America's greatest curses today. From this tough-fibered plant, the narcotic hashish and marijuana are produced. Hemp was also used to make the rope that hanged the witches. At Gallows Hill, as the hangman tried to place the noose around Sussana Martin's neck, on July 19, 1692, she "uttered incantations" and "the noose wiggled and danced in the air," so said a frightened onlooker. People in the crowd, well versed in witchcraft, told the hangman that he should use "willow withe" and not hemp for the noose. Willow withe, these learned witnesses realized, is immune to witchcraft. The hangman tried it, and it worked - Sussana Martin was successfully hanged.

A mere choking spasm, or even just a bad cough, was considered the result of a witch's evil touch. Any physical contact with a witch could cause blindness, even death, or worse than that, could make one fall in love with the wrong person, including the Devil himself. The children of Salem considered being touched by a witch, a real threatening force. When the accusing girls of Salem Village visited Andover to ferret out witches, they didn't know the names of anyone in town, which made their task the more difficult. The town fathers had all the local eccentrics, old hags, and those that had been acting strange, line up on the Common to touch each girl. When certain of these misfits touched the girls, "the children went into fits and vomitted trash". Some of the girls were, of course, play acting, but others probably went into fits of terror at being touched by a suspected witch. This may be the reason why there were more people from Andover accused of witchcraft, than from any other town or village in Essex County in 1692.

Even Doctor Griggs of Salem Village, when he could not find good cause for the girls' "unknown distempers", announced to the villagers that, "the evil hand is upon them". County doctors of the 17th century were often too quick in diagnosing an illness as being caused by a witch.

In those days, it was common knowledge that witches often knew more about folk medicine than doctors did. The name "witch" comes from theMedieval word "wicca", meaning "one who cures with magic". If one was suffering under pain and sickness from being touched by an evil witch or wizard, the cure was to be touched in turn by a good and pure person, preferably a minister of the Puritan Church. Cotton Mather was in great demand to sooth afflicted children with his touch. Robert Calef wrote that, "Mather quieted one teenaged girl by rubbing her stomach, her breast not covered with the bedclothes."

One superstition of New England folks, an offshoot of the witch's touch, was the ordeal of "Bier Right." It was a belief that lasted well into the 18th century. Bier Right, as it was termed in courts of law, was the capacity of a dead person to bleed when touched by his or her murderer, proving guilt. It was used in court as evidence in a murder case, when, and if, all other legal methods of determining guilt or innocence failed. It was also called, "the ordeal of touch". If the corpse bled when touched, the accused was guilty, but if the corpse did not bleed when the accused touched it, he or she was innocent. The last recorded murder trial in America, where Bier Right was to be the deciding evidence, was in 1769, in — of all places — Salem, Massachusetts.

Rebecca Ames had been condemned as a witch in Salem, in 1692. She escaped the hangman's noose, only because the Governor released all condemned witches from jail in the Spring of 1693, but she had languished too long in Salem's Witch Dungeon and was never well, physically or mentally, for the rest of her life. The Ames family could not forgive Thomas Perley, a neighbor and the captain of the jury at the witch trial. It was Perley, they said , who condemned poor Rebecca. Yet, when over half a century had passed, the families of Ames and Perley forgot their differences; John Ames of Boxford, Rebecca's grandson, married Ruth Perley of Topsfield, Thomas Perley's grandaughter. After a few years of what seemed to be a happy marriage, Ruth Perley Ames was found dead in her home. The doctor thought she had been poisoned. Her husband was arrested on the charge of murder, and John's mother was accused of being an accessory. There not being any substantial evidence that John Ames had poisoned his wife, he was asked to undergo the "ordeal of touch." If he refused, the jury would probably decide that his reluctance was due to guilt. If he touched the corpse of his wife and she bled, he would be hanged as a murderer, and if she didn't bleed, he - like his grandmother before him - would be accused of being a wizard, with the undeniable power of touch. John was damned if he did and damned if he didn't. His attorney, however intervened, refusing to allow his client to touch the body. The attorney accused the Salem Court of, "black arts and witchcraft." He then successfully defended John Ames, who, with his mother, was allowed to go free. Thus ended the power of witchcraft in Salem, 77 years after the 1692 hysteria.

There is, of course, that nagging doubt that maybe Bridget Bishop, Rebecca Ames, and yes even her grandson John Ames, were real witches. If John Ames was a witch or wizard, he certainly paid off the attorney that defended him with a powerful witch potion, for he went on to become the second President of the United States. John Ames' attorney was John Adams. Adams, as we all know, with Thomas Jefferson gave us The Declaration of Independence on July 4th, 1776. What some Americans might not realize is, both Presidents died exactly fifty years later, on July 4th, 1826. On his deathbed, John Adam's last words were, "Jefferson still lives"; unbeknownst to him, Jefferson, too, was dying — he left this world an hour after Adams died. So you see, witchcraft can be very powerful stuff, for those who believe.

This old wood cut reveals the power of witchcraft -
Do you see a pretty girl or a witch? — Look again.

VI

OLD HOLE IN THE HEAD

Phineas Gage scratched his head. It was a cool autumn afternoon, yet perspiration dripped down his neck. He was angry now, that he had decided to visit the old gypsy wagon to have his palm read. He had roared with laughter when the old hag tickled his fingers and said, "you will appear on the stage and become very rich for your performance. . . people will talk about you hundreds of years after your death." Phineas was not an actor, singer or dancer; why then would people pay to see him on stage, he wondered? The thought humored him and would surely bring a chuckle from his co-workers on the railroad construction gang. The fortune-telling witch also predicted that he would travel to far away places, yet Phineas had never left his New England home and had no desire to. "I've been had by a goofy old hag," he concluded as he stepped down from the wagon after paying her fifty cents, but one of her statements truly frightened him: "The icy fingers of death will touch you before sunset tomorrow", she had cackled.

Phineas returned to work next day at Covendish, Vermont, where he was construction foreman for the Rutland and Burlington Railroad. It was Saturday, September 13, 1848. "Lucky it's not Friday the 13th", one of his workers responded after he told his men about the old witch's predictions. "I wouldn't worry too much about it Phinney," laughed another, "cause if you was gonna die before night fall today, you sure as hell ain't gonna find time to travel around the world doing a step dance", "and you aint gonna become a millionaire on this job, that's for sure," piped up another. All through the morning, his men made snide yet playful comments to Phineas about the fortune teller. By noon, he had wished he hadn't mentioned his visit to the others.

By mid-afternoon, he felt he had been ridiculed enough. "We'll blow one last hole in the ledge boys and call it a day." The men cheered. Phineas was the expert at tamping down the blasting powder after the holes were drilled, so he ordered the drillers to back away as he tamped down the sand and powder with his special iron crowbar, made for him by the railroad blacksmith. Straddling the three-foot crowbar, Phineas turned around to make sure his men were at a proper distance before he gave the signal for the explosives to be set off. The crowbar slipped, causing a spark from the ledge which ignited the powder. There was a tremendous explosion, which carried rocks and dust high into the air. Phineas Gage was the only one near enough to the blast to be injured. When the cloud cleared his men saw him lying on his back, covered with blood. They thought he was dead, but Phineas groaned and moved his head. As the men rushed towards him, he shakily got to his feet. His clothes and hands were burned, and blood gushed from his cheek and head. The men tied cloth to his head to stop the flow of blood, and helped him to a nearby oxcart. During the mile ride to the doctor's house in Covendish, Phineas told his men that his crowbar had been blown clear through his skull. This, thought they all, was impossible, yet the holes in his head could be explained no other way.

When Doctor Harlow cleaned the powder burns and blood that blackened Gage's face and head, he found a three inch hole below his left eye and another of the same size at the top of his skull. The doctor fit the fingers of his left hand into the hole in his cheek and pushed his right hand into the skull wound to remove bone silvers. To the doctor's surprise the fingers of both hands touched inside Phineas' head. The three-foot long crowbar had indeed entered his head below the left eye and was blown clear through his skull. Although Phineas lost the sight of his left eye, there were no other effects from the wound and he was up and walking around within a week.

To the doctor, his friends and relatives, who all were convinced that no man could live through such an experience, he chuckled and said, "I didn't have much of a brain before, but I only got half a brain now". He, of course, kept the crowbar, but because of the loss of his eye the railroad company would not rehire him. He left for Boston, where - on the Common - he set up a tent and put himself and the crowbar on exhibition. P. T. Barnum then heard about Phineas and hired him for his New York museum, advertised as "The Only Living Man With a Hole in His Head".

For those skeptics who visited Barnum's sideshow, they were allowed to peek through the top of Phineas' skull to watch his brain pulsate. Phineas was also displayed at Harvard University, before doubting doctors and scientists, who, after studying his well-healed wounds, doubted no more. In fact, Phineas' skull can be seen at the medical museum at Harvard College today. When he finally died, 12½ years after the accident, Harvard had his body exhumed and the skull removed, in the interest of medical science.

Near the end of his days, Phineas became crude and boisterous, to the point that he was physically thrown out of Boston and New York sideshows. He traveled to Europe and South America, then settled in California, where his disposition remained menacing, and his well-polished 13½ pound crowbar remained at his side. Whether or not it was the skull wound that affected his personality, nobody knew.

The old crone fortune teller had been precise in her prediction, except for telling Phineas that he would become a profane egocentric. The question remains however, was it simply because of the accident itself, or did all that public attention just go to his head.

Home of the Marblehead Magician, John Dimond, and birthplace of famous Lynn mystic, Molly Pitcher, at the foot of Old Burying Hill, Marblehead, Massachusetts.

VII

MOLLY PITCHER AND THE MARBLEHEAD MAGICIAN

The town of Marblehead and the city of Lynn, on the northern coast of Massachusetts, are noted for many things. The quaint town claims to be "the Birthplace of the American Navy," and "the Yachting Capital of the World". In its historic Abbot Hall hangs the famous painting "The Spirit of '76". The industrial city of Lynn, claims to be "the Birthplace of America's Shoe Industry and of the Jet Engine." Many famous people, such as General John Glover, Playwright Eugene O'Neill and Industrialist Lydia Pinkham, were born in or lived much of their lives in these two communities.

Few people realize, however, that Lynn and Marblehead, both bordering Salem, are duly noted for their fortune tellers and mystics. The controversial "Marblehead Wizard" - John Dimond, and Lynn's Molly Pitcher are the most prominent. During the Eighteenth and Nineteenth Centuries, they were known throughout the country for their supernatural powers and their revelations of things to come.

Edward "John" Dimond, a tall, lanky, moody man, lived in a modest colonial home at Little Harbor in Marblehead. Of his childhood little is known, only that he would go into deep trances that would last for days, worrying his parents to the point of fear that he was dying from some strange sickness. When his father died, John inherited some money with which he purchased a large section of woodland around the town's Old Burying Hill. For what purpose he bought this land, the locals did not know. It had been only 27 years since the Witch Trials, in neighboring Salem. and the people, still highly superstitious, said that John was practicing black magic in his newly acquired woodlands. If he had lived during the witch hysteria, he most certainly would have been accused, sent to jail, and probably executed for being a witch. In the early 1700's however, New Englanders were reluctant to persecute anyone with supernatural powers; so, instead of using the distasteful name of "witch", the locals referred to John Dimond as a "wizard".

When the Widow Brown, a poor elderly woman, complained that someone had stolen the firewood that she had painstakingly cut and stacked for the cold winter months ahead; it was John Dimond who went into one of his trances and was able to name the thief. Dimond then confronted the man who stole the wood "and so charmed him, that he was forced to walk the streets of the town all night with a heavy log on his back", said the locals of the day. Dimond probably insisted that the man carry the logs back to Widow Brown's house. John Dimond was many times called upon to find lost or stolen money and valuables. Although he did not have a 100% record of recovery, he did seem to possess the elementary investigative skills of a Sherlock Holmes. He also had the curious ability to foretell disasters, as well as an uncanny sense of predicting New England's ever changing weather. Before a storm would hit the coast, he would climb to the top of Old Burying Hill; his presence there would alert Marbleheaders of an approaching squall. He would then begin mumbling to the headstones, as if conferring with the bodies that lay beneath them. As the wind increased in intensity, so would the wizard's voice. Soon, those who listened from a considerable distance realized that he was directing ships of the Marblehead fishing fleet which were riding out the storm hundreds of miles at sea.

"Captain Smith of the ELIZABETH ANNE, do you hear me?" he would shout, "Keep to starboard four degrees run true to Halfway Rock." For hours, he would scream out commands from one skipper to another, calling them by name. If John Dimond disliked any skipper in the fishing fleet, God help that man during a storm, for John would curse and condemn him from amidst the gravestones. Ordinarily, one would think of John Dimond's ravings at the Burial Ground as a lot of hooplah from a madman, but the ships that would sail safely into Marblehead Harbor after the storm were always those that Dimond had directed; those he cursed, were consistantly lost at sea. A few skippers confessed that they had heard John's voice over the howling winds and hyp-notically followed his orders. What extra-sensory powers John Dimond had, nobody knows, but most of his accomplishments were for the good. The people of Marblehead adored and feared him. Today he is all but forgotten, except for the fact that the local high school sports teams are called "The Marblehead Magicians", in his memory. Occasionally, a local fisherman, after riding out a storm, will chuckle when congratulated on his seamanship, and reply, "Twern't me, twas John Dimond who done it."

John Dimond's grandaughter, Molly, was born at 42 Orne Street, Marblehead in 1738, directly across the road from "Old Burying Hill." Almost from the day she could walk, it was thought by her parents, that she had inherited the "abilities" of Sixth Sense from her grandfather. As a young girl, she could repeat conversations that her mother had had with neighbors and friends, even though young Molly had been away at school when her mother was having these talks. She could read the thoughts of her family and friends, which sometimes upset her parents, and often made friends avoid her like the plague. As a young girl, she predicted the war with Mother England and an American victory - which sent some of the Tories of Marblehead into fits of laughter. At age

22, she married Robert Pitcher of Marblehead and soon the couple moved to Lynn. Molly was not a pretty girl. She had a sad face with a long nose, thin lips and a rather large head for her slight build, but she had a wryness about her, which Robert Pitcher loved. He boasted to friends of her prophesies and fortune telling abilities, which, by 1770, led many people to the old Pitcher house, nestled at the foot of Lynn's famous "high rock". Some came to her for a lark, but those who did would leave with a serious expression on their palid faces. Molly would often tell them more about themselves than their own mothers knew. Mostly seamen came to see her before they would embark on a voyage. They knew Molly Pitcher would not humor them. If she saw their ship in distress, she would tell them. Many a schooner never left it's Massachusetts North Shore port for lack of a crew, due to Molly's prediction of doom. Like her grandfather, her miraculous powers of foretelling the future made her both a prominent and a feared person. When she died, at age 75, in 1813, she was known throughout the Country for her mystic influences. In fact, in 1832, John Greenleaf Whittier wrote a long poem about her and her powers of prediction.

Today, in Lynn, Massachusetts, there is a fortune teller who claims to be Molly Pitcher's great-great-great granddaughter. Upon returning to Massachusetts in 1960, after two years with the Army in Africa, I went to visit this woman. She was a pleasant, white-haired lady who invited me into her sitting room, but as I approached the doorway, she asked me to stop. She cocked her head as if listening to somebody speak, although I heard nothing, and there was no other person around. "Who is Francis?" she asked me. I thought for a moment and answered, "my father". His name was James Francis Cahill, but only his older friends and relatives called him "Francis". "He's very ill," said the old woman "and he should see a doctor". I felt a cold chill creep up my spine - the old woman was right. My father had not been feeling well and, at times, could hardly catch his breath. Even at my mother's constant pleadings, however, he would not see a doctor; he called them "all quacks". He didn't see a doctor until it was too late; he died of cancer a few years later. There was no way - at the time - that this fortune teller could have known who I was, what my father's name was, or in what condition he was. It was my first fortune telling experience and I was impressed. She then went on to tell me that I worked closely with a member of my family, and that my work had something to do with the sea. She was right again. I worked for my brother, who was President of New England Divers, an underwater salvage and sales business. She continued to act as though she was talking to some unseen spirit in the room; after questioning the spirit with, "What's that?" or "Say that again?" I sat silently in awe.

"You just returned from a long trip to somewhere far away".
"That's true", I replied.
"You did not like what you saw there - It disturbed you."
"Yes", I admitted. I was upset at the disease and poverty I witnessed in East Africa.

"Someone named Joe will have a great influence on your life", she said, but this prediciton, as yet, has not come to pass. I think it is rather ironic though, for, when I was a little boy, there was a fellow named "Joe" constantly at my side. I have no idea from where he came, but he was with me for years, to the point that my parents were worried. No one could see Joe but me, and even now I forget what he looked like. When people came to visit our home, I would scream when they were about to sit in an empty chair, because Joe was already sitting there. There was always an extra plate set at dinner for Joe, and my mother would have to tuck him into bed with me at night. My mother and her friends would humor me about Joe and they seemd to enjoy having him around, but my father decided not to tolerate him any longer, especially at the dinner table. Apparently it was my Uncle Phil Doherty who created Joe for me, for it was he who had the sorrowful duty to tell me that Joe had died. "He got hit by a car", I can vivdly remember my uncle telling me, when I was age ten. My parents were fed up with Joe, and since Uncle Phil had been responsible for bringing Joe into the world, it was his duty to get rid of him. To everyone's surprise, Joe's death did not seem to bother me; possibly, I myself was getting sick and tired of Joe. This could have been the Joe to whom the fortune teller was referring, but, of course, I must also consider the possibility that the fortune teller was full of baloney, and that probably Molly Pitcher wasn't her ancestor. She was, however, accurate in most of her statements and predictions.

Today, varying scientific names are given to what was once commonly considered "mysticism", or having a "sixth sense". Mind reading is called "telepathy"; the ability of the mind to move matter is called "psychokenesis"; "clairvoyance" is the word used to describe the ability of sensing that something is happening elsewhere-even though it may be happening hundreds or thousands of miles away; and to be able to predict something before it takes place is called "precognition." Most laymen and often scientists, themselves, lump all these unexplained phenomena into the term "E.S.P.",or "Extrasensory Perception". As we approach the 21st century, people with E.S.P. are no longer called mystics, magicians, or wizards. They are simply accepted as having an added ability or talent that most others do not possess. There are still, however, many critics of E.S.P. In fact, Massachusetts Attorney

General Edward Brooke was severely criticized, in the 1960's, for having Dutch psychic Peter Hurkos come to Boston to aid police in their search for the Boston Strangler. Yet Hurkos has been credited with finding hundreds of missing persons, and for solving 27 murders throughout the World, by merely going to the location of the tragedy and receiving mental impressions. At Hanscom, Massachusetts, the U.S. Air Force is conducting E.S.P. experiments as a possibility for advanced outerspace communications; but thus far the results have not been too promising.

There is hardly a person alive who has not experienced E.S.P. in one form or another. The real question is, however, "What causes it?" Do only certain people have E.S.P., or is it latent in all of us - and if so, Can it improve with practice or training?

Recently, a small mongrel dog named "Waggles," who lives in Dorchester, Massachusetts (seven miles from Boston), was applauded as "a four-legged mystic with E.S.P." The boy who owns Waggles was taken to Children's Hospital in Boston for a minor operation. The boy and the dog are very close, so Waggles was kept in the house when the boy left for his two day stay in the hospital bed. When Waggles was let out of the house that evening for his nightly duties, he disappeared. Five hours later he was at the front door of Children's Hospital, managed to dodge the night clerk, eight times tried to bypass the nurses on duty, and was heading straight for his young master's hospital bed when he was captured. He was later driven the seven miles back to Dorchester. How did Waggles know the boy was in the hospital, and how did he find the hospital? You try to figure that one out, while I attempt to contact my long lost pal Joe. Possibly only he could shed light on such a mystery.

" . . . . And down the darkening coast
run the tumultuous surges,
And clap their hands and shout to you,
O Bells of Lynn!
Till from the shuddering sea,
with your wild incantations,
Ye summon up the spectral moon,
O Bells of Lynn!
And starteled at the sight,
like the weird woman of Endor,
Ye cry aloud, and then are still,
O Bells of Lynn."
(The Bells of Lynn - By Henry Wadsworth Longfellow)

VIII
RHODE ISLAND'S PRETTY MYSTIC

Jemima Wilkinson was born only 13 years after Lynn's famous Molly Pitcher, in Cumberland, Rhode Island, one of 12 children. Unlike Molly, Jemima made a small fortune on her predictions, and, unlike Molly, few of her predictions ever were realized.

When Jemima was eight years old, her mother died having her thirteenth child; this loss profoundly effected the little girl. She was, by far, the most beautiful of the Wilkinson children, and she thrived on the attention little boys and cooing adults would give her. She disliked anything that would make her dirty, and thus she shirked all housework, usually faining some kind of sickness. When she became an adult, men pursued her with passion, but none of them suited her. At age 26 she was still unmarried and most of the local men had given up trying. Apparently this slump in attention distressed Jemima, so one evening she went to her bedroom where she remained for two years.

At first, she told her friends and family that she was sick. Then, after reading and rereading the Bible while lounging in bed, she announced that angels had visited her, periodically, and had chosen her to do miraculous deeds for the good of mankind. The local minister became interested in her visitors from heaven, and asked Jemima if she would care to preach a sermon on her experiences, at one of the Sunday services. She accepted, and her first miracle was getting out of bed after two years.

At the church meeting, the seemingly shy, beautiful young lady, with long flowing strawberry-blonde hair, was called to the pulpit. She began by telling the congregation of how she had gone into a trance for three days, during which time she had had many visions. One spirit, she said, told her that she would live for 1,000 years; and another revealed that she would become the leader of spiritual affairs in America.

She was the prettiest preacher anyone had ever seen, and she had a good speaking voice. Her audience loved her and she was invited as guest speaker to other congregations throughout Rhode Island. Her first prediction came true only a few weeks after getting out of bed. At East Greenwich, she stated to a gathering of 35 people, "one of you within the sound of my voice will not live another day". That night, a black servant boy who had heard Jemima speak doubled up in pain and dropped dead. Although a neighbor was accused of poisoning the boy, Jemima got all the credit.

Moving across the state border into Swansea, Massachusetts, Jemima announced that she would walk upon the waters at Mount Hope Bay. Thousands came to witness the miracle, but when this thinly clad beauty made the attempt, she, of course, went under. The crowd roared and jeered, as she emerged soaking wet and angry. She called them all "servants of the Devil" and "disbelievers". She and her few loyal followers returned to Rhode Island.

Realizing the need for money to continue in her service to Mankind, she befriended Judge William Potter, who owned a mansion called "Old Abbey" in southern Rhode Island. Jemima and her "Jemimakins", as her followers were now called, moved in with the Judge. The Judge's young daughter was terribly ill and Jemima promised to cure her. When the girl died, she promised to bring her back from the dead. Once again Jemima failed. By the time the Judge had become wise to her fakery, she had finagled thousands of dollars from him - enough to build two meeting houses in Rhode Island.

Jemima rode a white stallion as she traveled from town to town preaching and predicting. She also wore a long woolen cape, literally pulling the wool over the eyes of skeptics who confronted her. She was not only beautiful but gained the reputation of a "spitfire", who would just as soon strike a man or woman down as to look at them.

She and her followers did more than pull the wool over the Rhode Island State Treasurer's eyes. While staying overnight at his home, some of the Jemimakins managed to walk away with a couple of thousand dollars of the State Treasury the next morning. They fled with Jemima to Pennsylvania, but state investigators followed. When the investigators caught up with Jemima, they found $800 of the stolen money in her suitcase. Jemima then fled to upstate New York, where, with the remainder of the stolen money, she purchased a large parcel of land. On the land she built a plush home, started a farm and had the Jemimakins wait on her hand and foot. She was strict with her followers, who now numbered about 50, and any girl who was too pretty, she banned from her compound, which was called "Little Jerusalem". She reigned as queen of "Little Jerusalem," and it might be said that she lived happily ever after. Like most of her predictions, however, the 1,000 years of longevity she prophesized did not come true either. With still 932 years to go, she died in 1819 at the age of 68.

IX

THE HARVARD CONNECTION

There is little doubt that the Salem witch hysteria was influenced by the Mathers, Increase and Cotton, father and son, both Puritan ministers. Writers throughout the last three centuries have either blamed them, especially Cotton, for the hanging of innocent people, or concluded that they were heroes. David K. Wilson, in his article "The Forgotten Witches Of Boston," (Yankee Magazine, June, 1979) writes: "If there is a hero of the witchcraft delusion in Boston, that hero is Cotton Mather. He at least was able to contain it." Cotton Mather was a brilliant, sincere, God-fearing fanatic, who was a student at Harvard College when he was 12 years old, and head of Boston's Old North Church before he was 25. A year later, in 1689, he wrote and had published, "Memorable Providences, Relating to Witchcraft and Possessions," in which he resolves, "never to use but just one grain of patience with any man that shall go to impose upon me a denial of devils or of witches." Considered by most ministers and statesmen of New England to be the authority on the subject of witches and wizards, Cotton willingly accepted the challenge of ferreting out "these rampant hags" and took on as his personal crusade, revealing "the plot of the Devil against New England." He wrote that, "so horrid and hellish is the crime of witchcraft that were God's thoughts as our thoughts, or God's way as our ways, it could be no other but unpardonable." In his lectures, sermons, and writings, he aroused the superstitions and fears of the Colonists, and instilled courage and enthusiasm in the other ministers to do battle with the army of demons that invaded Salem in 1692.

When John Harvard, of Charlestown, died in 1639, he left half his fortune and 300 volumes to build America's first college. Harvard was to be built at Salem, but Boston politicians prevailed and Harvard was built across Boston's Charles River at Cambridge. That same year, Increase Mather was born; 17 years later, he graduated from Harvard. He continued his schooling at Trinity College, Dublin, Ireland, and became minister in England until 1661, when he returned to America. The following year, his son Cotton was born. Increase was a distinguished Puritan clergyman in Boston and Cambridge, and, during the Salem witch hysteria, was President of Harvard College. His preachings and writings had a strong influence on his son. He wrote about ghosts and witches, and was continuously trying to entice skeptics into believing in the supernatural. In 1684, Increase wrote and published, "An Essay For The Recording Of Illustrious Providence." It was all about witchcraft and demonic possessions; in it he showed the reader many ways to recognize the works of the Devil. In one of his stories, "The Drummer Of Tedworth - March 1662 to April, 1663", he tells about William Drury, who had been a drummer in the British Army and had become a vagrant. He was brought before a Judge Mompesson of Tedworth, who put Drury behind bars, at Salisbury Jail, because he was always dancing around the village beating his drum and making a nuisance of himself. It was also thought that Drury had stolen a pig in Gloucester; and for that, Judge Mompesson was ready to banish him to Virginia. The most horrid punishment for Drury however, was that the Judge had taken away his drum. To get even with Mompesson, according to Mather, Drury bewitched the drum, which the judge had placed in his own home. "The noise of thumping and drumming was very frequent," wrote Mather, "usually five nights together, on the outside of the house" and "constantly came as they (the judge and his wife) were going to sleep . . . and then from the room where the drum was." Drury was tried and condemned as a witch. Although Increase Mather seemingly saw no travisty of justice in this, he also said that he was opposed to using spectral evidence to convict people of witchcraft. "It is better that ten suspected witches should escape," he wrote, "than that one honest person should be condemned . . . I'd rather judge a witch to be an honest woman, than judge an honest woman as a witch."

Cotton Mather, in his book "Memorable Provinces," in 1689, also wrote, "Take heed that you do not wrongfully accuse any other person of this horrid and monstrous evil," yet he did just that, three years later. At the Salem trial of Martha Carrier, one of three sisters condemned as witches, he wrote, "this rampant hag was the person of whom the confessions of the witches, and of her own children, (after being tortured in the Witch Dungeon) among the rest, agreed that the devil had promised her that she should be the queen of hell."

In May of 1692, when the new Governor, Phips, arrived in Boston from England, over 160 accused witches were already in jail, and the Colonies were in a witch-panic. The French and Indians were also stirring up trouble on the Canadian border. Increase Mather sailed across the Atlantic with Phips. By the time they reached New England, Mather had convinced the Governor that he should personally handle the French and Indians, and that he should set up a special court to handle the witch problem, appointing Deputy Governor Soughton - "the savage Stoughton" - as chief magistrate. Less than a month passed, when this special (illegal) court, after hearing evidence condemning Salem's Bridget Bishop, turned to Cotton Mather for answers as to what to do from that point on. Mather replied in writing to the magistrates, on June 15, 1692:

"In the prosecution of these witches and all such witchcraft, there is need of a very critical and exquisite caution . . . that all proceedings be managed with an exceeding tenderness toward those that may be complained of, especially if they have been persons formerly of an unblemished reputation . . . ." If Cotton Mather had ended his letter right there, we probably would never have heard of the hangings of Salem Witches, but he went on in his letter of instruction to the judges: "tis an undoubted and a notorious thing that a Demon may, by God's permission, appear even to ill purposes in the shape of an innocent, yea, and a virtuous man. Nevertheless, we cannot but humbly recommend unto the government the speedy and vigorous prosecution of such as have rendered themselves obnoxious, according to the direction given in the Laws of God and the wholesome statutes of the English nation for the detection of witchcraft."

Cotton Mather even attended one of the gruesome mass hangings at Salem's Gallows Hill, on August 19, 1692, where onlookers pleaded with him to save the life of Maine clergyman, George Burroughs. Knowing that Burroughs was convicted on hearsay and specter evidence, Mather watched him dangle from the gallows. "The devil is most dangerous when appearing as an angel of light," Mather told the crowd. George Burroughs was not only a minister of the Puritan church, but also, like Mather, a graduate of Harvard College.

"Wonders Of The Invisible World," was written by Cotton Mather in 1693. Its subtitle was, "an account of the sufferings brought upon the great crisis in religion," and yet it was he who continued to fan Satan's flames to kindle this crisis.

A few Colonials had courage enough to question the Mathers and their beliefs. As early as October, 1692, Thomas Brattle, of Boston, published and circulated a letter in which he asked: "Why do the witches afflict only some girls and no others? Why are confessions full of lies and flat contradictions accepted by the court? Why are highly placed persons who are accused of witchcraft (such as Margaret Thatcher, the mother-in-law of Judge Corwin) not prosecuted? No one answered these questions for Tom Brattle, and Cotton Mather was outraged that he should even ask them. Three months later, the witch judges in Salem decided not to accept spectral evidence, as they began their first session of 1693, the jails overflowing with witches. They did, however, ask Mather again, "How much weight should be given it?"

They were answered by a clothing merchant of Harvard Square, Robert Calef, who said, "As much as the weight of chips in beer."

Another book, "More Wonders Of The Invisible World," was written by Robert Calef, who had witnessed the hangings and the crushing of Giles Corey in Salem, but, although no one in America would print it, he had it printed by Nathaniel Hillar of London, England. Calef's book denounced Cotton Mather's book on witches, and became an immediate best-seller in the Colonies. Calef not only depicted Cotton Mather as a demented witch hunter, but suggested that he was immoral when he went into rooms alone with young women to touch them in an effort to drive out demons from their bodies. Calef, an uneducated man, did a remarkable job in thoroughly discrediting Mather. Cotton wrote and published a rebuttal in 1701, titled, "Some Few Remarks Upon A Scandalous Book," but it was too little too late. Increase Mather had Calef's book publicy burned in Harvard Yard.

Book burning is a scandal in itself; 280 years later, on February 18, 1983, the President of Harvard University, Derek Bok, at a special dinner meeting at Harvard, publicy apologized for the book burning incident and paid $10 in recompense to Oliver Brown, assistant superintendent of schools in Cambridge. Robert Calef is a direct ancestor of Brown's, through his father's mother. Brown commented to the dinner guests that, "not only were Increase and Cotton Mather tormented by Calef's book, but that Calef himself was so bothered and pestered by local ministers who were friends of the Mathers, that he was forced to leave Cambridge and live the rest of his life in Roxbury." Brown also said that, after consulting with his son, Calef Robert Brown, they decided to donate the $10 from the Harvard President to the nuclear freeze movement.

What the President of Harvard and most others do not realize, is that Cotton Mather instigated a terrible curse on that great college, causing Harvard's faculty, students, and alumni, such suffering and pain over the centuries, that a witch's curse would seem tame in comparison.

Because of Calef's book, Cotton Mather was passed over as President of Harvard, even though his father had seen to it that he should be next in line for the job. This was probably Cotton's greatest disappointment in life. Neverthless, until he died, at age 66, in 1758, he continued to write about and uphold his beliefs in witches and witchcraft. Another complaint of his, revealed in his diary, is that throughout the remainder of life, "on purpose, to affront me, some call their negroes by the name,

Cotton Mather." Cotton got even with Harvard though. For the affront at not making him President, he persuaded one of his wealthy English friends to fund and found a new college in America. Mather made himself its President. "It is to be more conservative than Harvard," said Mather. He decided to locate the college in New Haven, Connecticut and named it after his generous English friend, Elihu Yale. . . . A never ending curse to the Crimson Tide of Harvard. Mather's new college however, seems to be the only good thing that came out of the Salem Witch hysteria.

Cotton Mather,
Essex Institute, Salem, Massachusetts

- A Book Of New England Legends And Folklore, By Samuel Adams Drake, Charles E. Tuttle Company, Rutland, Vermont — 1884 & 1971.
- The Devil In Massachusetts, By Marion L. Starkey, Alfred A. Knopf, Inc. — 1950.
- More Yankee Yarns, Alton H. Blackington, Dodd, Mead & Company, New York — 1956.
- Sketch of Salem 1626 - 1879, By Charles S. Osgood and H.M. Batchelder, Salem Essex Institute — 1879.
- Witchcraft Magic And Alchemy, By Grillot De Givry, Translated By J. Courtenay Locke, Houghton Mifflin Company — 1931.
- The Story Of Essex County, Compiled By Scott H. Paradise, The American Historical Society, Inc. , New York — 1935.
- Records Of Salem Witchcraft, Burt Franklin, New York, Published By Lenox Hill Co., N.Y. — 1864 & 1972.
- Mysterious New England, Edited By Austin N. Stevens, Published By Yankee, Inc., Dublin N.H. — 1971.
- The Encyclopedia Of Witchcraft And Demonology, By Russell Hope Robbins, Crown Publishers, Inc., N.Y. — 1959.
- Witchcraft At Salem, By Chadwick Hansen, The New American Library, Inc. — Times Mirror, N.Y. — 1969.
- Chronicles Of Old Salem, Frances Diane Robotti, Bonanza Books, New York — 1948.
- Irish Witchcraft & Demonology, By St. John D. Seymour B.D. — Causeway Books, N.Y. — 1973.
- Witches And Witchcraft, By Jeremy Kingston, The Danbury Press, Grolier Enterprises, Inc. — 1976.
- Psychic — The Story Of Peter Hurkos, By Peter Hurkos, The Bobbs-Merril Co., Inc., N.Y. — 1961.
- Old Landmarks And Historic Personages Of Boston, By Samuel Drake Adams, Boston — 1906.
- Chronicles Of Danvers (Old Salem Village) Massachusetts 1623 — 1923, Danvers, Mass. — 1923.
- Essex County Archives, Salem Witchcraft, Essex Institute, Salem, Mass. — 1692.
- Pathways Of The Puritans, By The Secretary Of The Commonwealth Of Mass., Plimpton Press, Norwood, Mass. — 1930.